COOL

PAPER FOLDING

CREATIVE ACTIVITIES THAT MAKE MATH & SCIENCE
FUN FOR KIDS!

ANDERS HANSON

A Division of ABDO
ABDO
Publishing Company

AND ELISSA MANN

VISIT US AT WWW.ABDOPUBLISHING.COM

Published by ABDO Publishing Company, a division of ABDO, P.O. Box 398166, Minneapolis, Minnesota 55439. Copyright ® 2014 by Abdo Consulting Group, Inc. International copyrights reserved in all countries. No part of this book may be reproduced in any form without written permission from the publisher. Checkerboard Library™ is a trademark and logo of ABDO Publishing Company.

Printed in the United States of America, North Mankato, Minnesota
062013
012014

♻ PRINTED ON RECYCLED PAPER

Design and Production: Anders Hanson, Mighty Media, Inc.
Series Editor: Liz Salzmann
Photo Credits: Anders Hanson, Shutterstock

LIBRARY OF CONGRESS CATALOGING-IN-PUBLICATION DATA

Hanson, Anders.
 Cool paper folding : creative activities that make math & science fun for kids! / Anders Hanson and Elissa Mann.
    p. cm. -- (Cool art with math & science)
 Includes bibliographical references and index.
 ISBN 978-1-61783-823-1
1. Paper work--Juvenile literature. 2. Origami--Juvenile literature. 3. Handicraft--Juvenile literature. I. Mann, Elissa, 1990- II. Title.
 TT870. H3139 2014
 736.98--dc23
                    2013001899

CONTENTS

COOL
PAPER FOLDING

How many different things can you make by folding paper? You might be surprised. Many kids make paper airplanes and boats. But you can also make things such as cubes, tetrahedrons, and **ninja** stars. Get ready to go on a paper-folding adventure!

The Japanese have been folding paper for hundreds of years. They call it *origami*. Most origami projects look like animals.

Modern paper folding artists create colorful art using only folded paper.

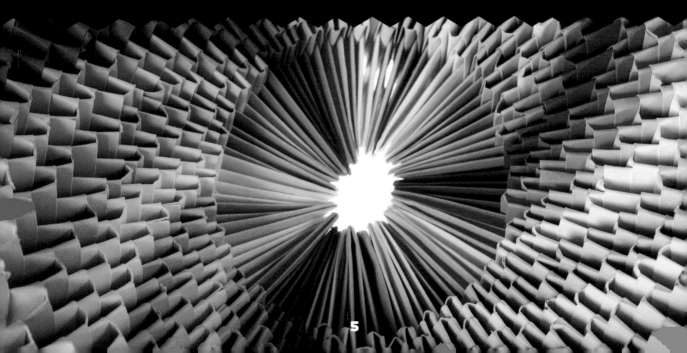

Folding paper can be fun. It can also be challenging. With some practice, you will be a paper folding pro.

ORIGAMI PAPER

Use **origami** paper for paper-folding projects. It is available at craft stores. It is lighter than regular paper. This makes it easy to fold. Most origami paper is 6 inches by 6 inches (15.24 cm by 15.24 cm).

FOLDING TIPS

» Be as **accurate** as possible when you make your folds! Make sure to crease the folds.

» Be patient. It can take a few tries to get it right.

» Read the directions and look at the pictures carefully. If you don't understand something, ask a friend or an adult for help.

REGULAR POLYGONS
THE ESSENTIAL SHAPES

A polygon is a shape. Its sides are straight lines. In a regular polygon, all the sides are the same length. And all the corners have the same angle.

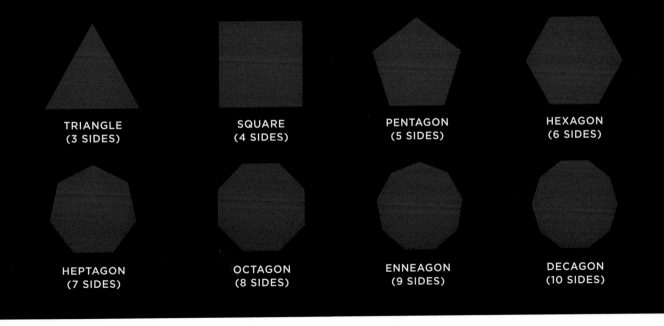

THE FIRST EIGHT REGULAR POLYGONS

TRIANGLE
(3 SIDES)

SQUARE
(4 SIDES)

PENTAGON
(5 SIDES)

HEXAGON
(6 SIDES)

HEPTAGON
(7 SIDES)

OCTAGON
(8 SIDES)

ENNEAGON
(9 SIDES)

DECAGON
(10 SIDES)

PLATONIC SOLIDS
THE REGULAR POLYHEDRONS

A platonic solid is a three-dimensional shape. It is also called a polyhedron. Its faces are regular polygons. Each face is the same.

There are five platonic solids. They are the tetrahedron, the cube, the octahedron, the dodecahedron, and the icosahedron.

Make each solid by folding a sheet of paper. The pattern for each solid is shown on the right. The dotted lines are tabs for gluing or taping.

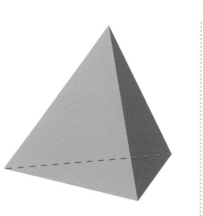

TETRAHEDRON

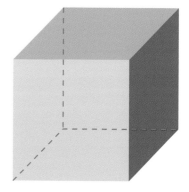

CUBE

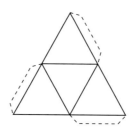

MADE FROM
4 TRIANGLES

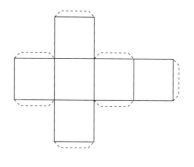

MADE FROM
6 SQUARES

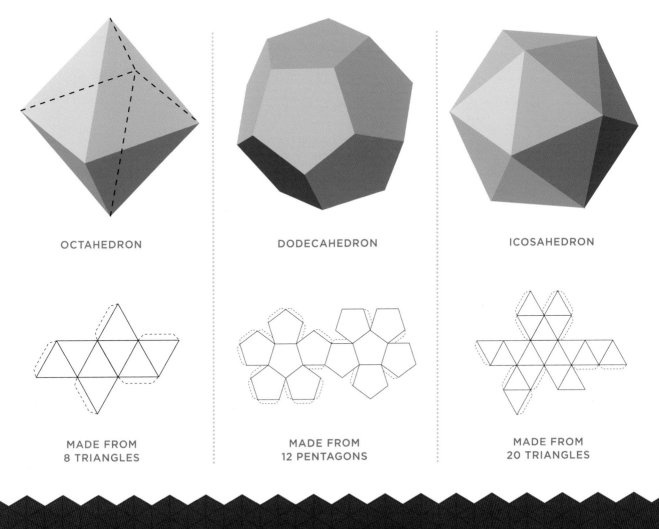

OCTAHEDRON

DODECAHEDRON

ICOSAHEDRON

MADE FROM
8 TRIANGLES

MADE FROM
12 PENTAGONS

MADE FROM
20 TRIANGLES

ICOSAHEDRON

OCTAHEDRON

TETRAHEDRON

PROJECT

1 FOLDING A PLATONIC SOLID

◆◆◆◆◆◆◆◆

STUFF YOU'LL NEED

- CARD STOCK
- COLORED PAPER
- RULER
- PEN OR PENCIL
- TAPE
- SCISSORS

TERMS

- TETRAHEDRON
- FACE
- EQUILATERAL TRIANGLE
- MIDPOINT

The tetrahedron is the simplest platonic solid. It has four faces. Each face is an equilateral triangle.

The steps show how to fold a piece of paper into a tetrahedron. Make the other platonic solids using the same method. See pages 8–9 for the folding patterns.

HOW TO MAKE IT

1 Use a ruler to draw a 3-inch (7.6 cm) line on card stock. This is the base of the triangle.

2 Measure 1.5 inches (3.8 cm) in from one end of the line. This is the midpoint. Use the corner of a piece of paper to draw a line up from the midpoint. It should be at least 3 inches (7.6 cm) long.

3 Draw a 3-inch (7.6 cm) line from each end of the base line to the midpoint line. This will form a triangle.

4 Cut out the triangle. You will use it as a **template**.

5 Trace the template on a piece of colored paper.

6 Trace three more triangles using the **template**. Each triangle should share a side with the first triangle. All the triangles will form one big triangle.

7 Cut out the big triangle.

8 Fold each outer triangle in. Crease them along the lines they share with the center triangle.

9 Lift up two triangles. Tape their edges together.

10 Put tape on the other edge of both triangles. Press the edges of the third triangle to the tape. This completes the solid tetrahedron.

PROJECT 2

MAKING A NINJA STAR

> ### STUFF YOU'LL NEED

- 2 PIECES OF ORIGAMI PAPER

> ### TERMS

- TRIANGLE
- VERTICAL

Have you ever seen **ninjas** in a movie? Ninjas carry tiny metal stars in their pockets. They throw the stars at their targets. You can make your own ninja star, too! Try making this paper **version**.

Tip: It's important to make firm creases. Make sure you fold as **accurately** as possible!

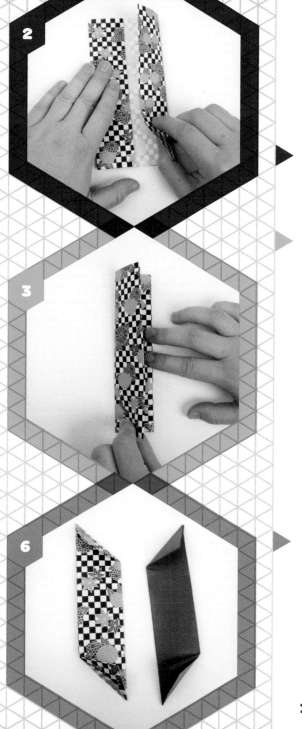

HOW TO MAKE IT

1 Lay the paper facedown. Fold it in half. Make a firm crease. Unfold it.

2 Fold one side of the paper to the center crease. Crease it. Repeat with the other side.

3 Leave the sides folded in. Fold the paper on the center crease.

4 Repeat steps 1 through 3 with a second piece of paper.

5 Lay them down with the folds on the left. Fold the top right corner of the first paper down. Line up the corner with the left edge. Fold the top left corner of the second paper down. Line up the corner with the right edge.

6 Fold the bottom left corner of the first paper up. Line up the corner with the right edge. Fold the bottom right corner of the second paper up. Line up the corner with the left edge.

7 On the first paper, fold the left edge of the top half to the center. The top point should be on the right side. Fold the right edge of the bottom half to the center. The bottom point should be on the left side. The folds will make two triangles with pockets. Fold the top and bottom of the second paper the opposite way.

8 Flip the first paper over. Turn it so it's vertical. Place the second paper on top. Do not flip it over.

9 Fold the bottom right corner up. Tuck it into the left triangle pocket. Fold the top left corner down. Tuck it into right triangle pocket.

10 Flip the papers over. Tuck in the other corners the same way.

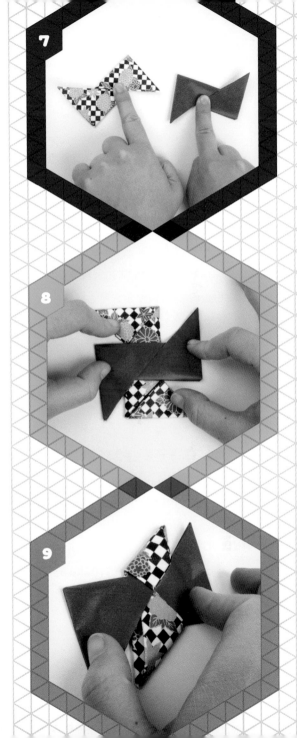

MODULES
BITS AND PIECES PUT TOGETHER

Modules are pieces that fit together. They can be mixed and matched to make something larger. Modules can always be separated and put back together in a different way. They are like building blocks!

Some **origami** projects are made with folded modules. It is called modular origami. The projects on pages 20 and 24 use modules.

REAL LIFE MODULES

A brick is an example of a real-life module. Bricks are mostly the same size and shape. When you put them together, they can make a lot of things. Bricks can make a house, a road, or an arch!

The Colosseum is an ancient **stadium** in Rome. It was built with bricks. In the 1300s an earthquake destroyed part of it. Many bricks broke off. They didn't go to waste, though. Because bricks are modular, they were reused in other buildings!

PROJECT

3

MAKING A MODULAR CUBE

◆◆◆◆◆◆◆

In modular **origami**, many **identical** pieces are put together. They make a new shape.

In this project, you will make six identical **modules**. Then you'll join them together to make a cube!

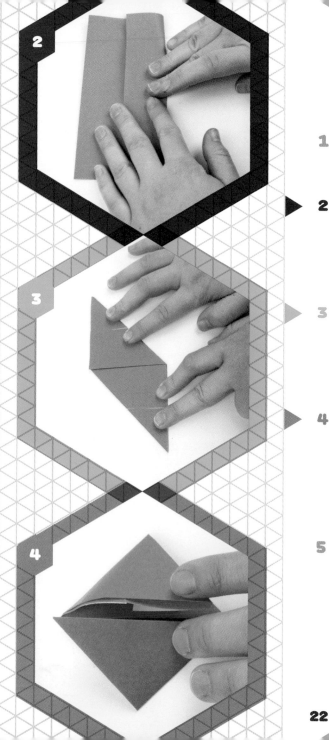

HOW TO MAKE IT

1 Fold a piece of paper in half. Make a firm crease. Unfold it.

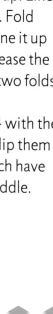 2 Fold one side of the paper to the center crease. Crease it. Repeat with the other side. Flip the paper over.

3 Fold the right top corner down. Line it up with the left edge. Fold the left bottom corner up. Line it up with the right edge.

4 Fold the bottom corner up. Line it up along the left edge. Fold the top corner down. Line it up along the right edge. Crease the folds. Open up the last two folds.

5 Repeat steps 1 though 4 with the other sheets of paper. Flip them all over. They should each have a diagonal **slot** in the middle.

6 Lay one folded paper horizontally. Slide one point of the second paper into the first paper's **slot** from the top. Slide one point of the third paper into the slot from the bottom.

7 Flip the three connected papers over. Fold up the second and third papers. They should stick up on either side of the first paper.

8 Hold the fourth paper between the raised ends of the second and third papers. Fold the point of the second paper over the fourth paper and into its slot. Do the same with the point of the third paper.

9 Add the last two papers to the sides the same way. Fold the points over and tuck them into the slots from the outside.

23

PROJECT

4

FOLDING A COMPLEX SHAPE

STUFF YOU'LL NEED

- SCISSORS
- 3 SHEETS OF ORIGAMI PAPER (DIFFERENT COLORS)
- PEN

TERMS

- SQUARE
- TRIANGLE
- POLYHEDRON
- RECTANGLE
- HORIZONTAL

This cool shape is made out of squares and triangles. It is not a polyhedron. That's because it isn't a solid. It has holes in it!

This piece was designed by Japanese **origami** master Tomoko Fuse. You can become a folding master too!

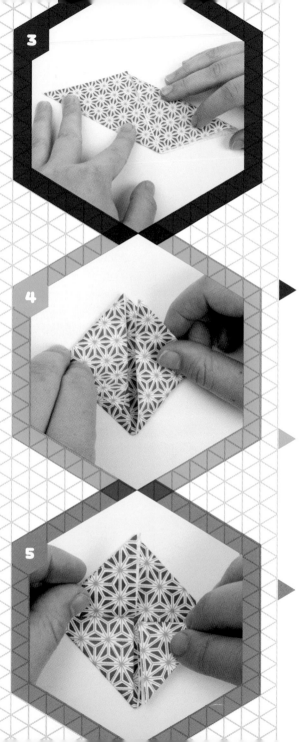

HOW TO MAKE IT

1   Fold three squares of paper in half. Cut each sheet in half on its fold. This creates six rectangles.

2   Lay one rectangle facedown horizontally.

3   Bring the bottom left corner up to meet the top edge. Fold it so the left edge is even with the top edge. Bring the top right corner down to the bottom edge. Fold it so the right edge is even with the bottom edge.

4   Fold the top left corner down. Line the corner up with the bottom corner to the left. Fold the bottom right corner up. Line up the corner with the top corner to the right. The folded paper will have two flaps.

5   Fold the right flap down over the bottom right half. Fold the left flap up over the top left half. Each flap has two **slots**. One at the tip and one at the base.

6 Repeat steps 2 through 5 for the remaining rectangles.

7 Flip them all over. Label them with the letters A through F.

8 Pull out the left flap of A. Put the tip of the flap into the base **slot** of B's right flap. Put the tip of B's right flap into the base slot of C's left flap. Put the tip of C's left flap into the base slot of A's left flap.

9 Put the tip of D's left flap into the base slot of A's right flap. Put the tip of B's left flap into the base slot of D's right flap.

10 Put the tip of A's right flap into the base **slot** of E's left flap. Put the tip of E's left flap into the base slot of D's left flap.

11 Put the tip of D's right flap into the base slot of F's left flap. Put the tip of F's left flap into the base slot of B's left flap.

12 Put the tip of C's right flap into the base slot of F's right flap. Put the tip of F's right flap into the base slot of E's right flap. Put the tip of E's right flap into the base slot of C's right flap.

MATH AND BEAUTY
IS THERE A CONNECTION?

Mathematics and beauty have been linked together for hundreds of years. Many consider mathematical objects, such as platonic solids, to be beautiful. What do you think?

"Mathematics, rightly viewed, possesses not only truth, but supreme beauty."
—BERTRAND RUSSELL

JACOPO DE' BARBARI,
PORTRAIT OF LUCA PACIOLI, 1500

LEONARDO DA VINCI,
UNTITLED,
1509

THE GREAT PYRAMIDS AT GIZA

MATH TERMS

CUBE - a 3-D shape with six square faces.

DIAGONAL - from one corner of a square or rectangle to the opposite corner.

EQUILATERAL TRIANGLE - a triangle with sides that are all the same length.

FACE - a polygon that forms one of the flat surfaces of a 3-D shape.

HORIZONTAL - in the same direction as the ground, or side-to-side.

MIDPOINT - the middle of a line.

POLYHEDRON - a 3-D shape with flat faces and straight edges.

RECTANGLE - a 2-D shape with four sides and four right angles.

SQUARE - a shape with four straight, equal sides and four equal angles.

TETRAHEDRON - a 3-D shape that has four faces.

TRIANGLE - a shape with three straight sides.

VERTICAL - in the opposite direction from the ground, or up-and-down.

GLOSSARY

ACCURATE - exact or correct.

IDENTICAL - exactly the same.

MODULE - one of a group of similar pieces that can be used together.

NINJA - a person trained in ancient Japanese martial arts.

ORIGAMI - the Japanese art of paper folding.

SLOT - a narrow opening.

STADIUM - a large building with an open area for sporting events surrounded by rows of seats.

TEMPLATE - a shape you draw or cut around to copy it onto something else.

VERSION - a different form or type from the original.

WEB SITES

To learn more about math and science, visit ABDO Publishing Company on the World Wide Web at www.abdopublishing.com. Web sites about creative ways for kids to experience math and science are featured on our Book Links page. These links are routinely monitored and updated to provide the most current information available.

INDEX